D1454939

Jonas going to Market.

ROLLO

LEARNING TO READ.

Abbott

THE ROLLO SERIES

IS COMPOSED OF FOURTEEN VOLUMES, VIZ.

A NEW EDITION, REVISED BY THE AUTHOR.

PHILADELPHIA:
PUBLISHED BY HOGAN & THOMPSON.

BOSTON:
GOULD, KENDALL & LINCOLN.
1850.

NOTICE TO PARENTS.

In those intervals of rest which the serious cares and labors of life imperiously demand, a man may find the best amusement for himself in efforts for the amusement of children. This little work and its predecessor, "ROLLO LEARNING TO TALK," have been written on this principle.

Parents find it very difficult to *employ* little children. "Mother, what shall I do?" and sometimes even, "Mother, what shall I do after I have done this?" are heard so often that they sometimes exhaust even maternal patience. These little volumes will, we hope, in some cases, provide an answer to the questions. The writer has endeavored to make them such that children would take an interest in reading them to themselves, and to their younger brothers and sisters, and in repeating them to one another.

The difficulty with most books intended for children just learning to read, is, that the writers make so much effort to confine themselves to *words of one syllable*, that the style is quaint and unin-

1*

teresting, and often far more unintelligible than the
usual language would be. The author's design here
has been, first to interest the little reader, hoping,
by this interest, to allure him on to the encounter
of the difficulties in the language, and to the con-
quest of them.   Hence the more difficult words and
phrases, in common use, are not *avoided*, for the
very object of such a reading book should be to
teach the use of them.   They are freely introduced,
and rendered intelligible by being placed in strik-
ing connections, and familiar, by being frequently
repeated.   By a wonderful provision in the struc-
ture of the mind, children thirst for repetition ;—the
very thing essential to give security and perma-
nence to the knowledge they acquire.

   The subjects of the articles, accordingly, and the
method of treating them, are in the highest degree
juvenile.   But the language is mature.   For it is
language which we wish to teach them, and con-
sequently we must keep, in language, a little above
them, advancing continually ourselves, as *they* ad-
vance.   J. A.

   Roxbury, Nov. 5, 1835.

CONTENTS.

HOW ROLLO LEARNED TO READ.

SHOULD you like to know how Rollo learned to read? I will tell you. It is very hard work to learn to read, and it takes a great while to do it. I will tell you how Rollo did it.

One evening Rollo was sitting on the floor by the side of the fire, playing with his blocks. He was trying to build a meeting-house. He could make the meeting-house very well, all except the steeple, but the steeple *would* tumble down.

Presently his father said,

"Rollo, you may put your blocks into the basket, and put the basket in its place, in the closet, and then come to me."

Rollo obeyed.

Then Rollo's father took him up into his lap, and took a little book out of his pocket. Rollo was glad. He thought he was going to look at some pictures. But he was disappointed.

He was disappointed,—that is he found there were no pictures in the book, and was sorry.

His father said,

"I suppose you thought there were pictures in this book."

"Yes sir," said Rollo.

"There are none," said his father; "I have not got this book to amuse you. I am going to have you learn to read out of it, and learning to read is hard work."

Rollo was very glad when he heard this. He wanted to learn to read, so that he could read story books himself alone, and he thought that learning to read was very pleasant, easy work.

His father knew that he thought so, and therefore he said,

"I suppose you are glad that you are going to learn to read, but it is harder work and will take longer time than you think. You will get tired very often, before you have learned, and you will want to stop. But you must not stop.

"What," said Rollo, "must not I stop once,—at all—all the time, till I have learned to read?"

"Oh yes," said his father; "I do not mean that you must be learning to read all the time ;—you will only read a little while every day. What I mean is that you must read every day, when the time comes, although you will very often think that you are tired of reading so much, and had rather play. But no matter if you are tired of it. It is your duty to learn to read and you must do it, if it is hard."

"I do not think I shall be tired," said Rollo.

"Very well,—you can see. Only remember if you should be tired, you must not say so, and ask not to read."

Rollo's father then opened the book and showed Rollo that it was full of letters,—large letters, and small letters, and a great many little words in columns. Do you know what a column is? There was also some very easy reading in large print, but no pictures.

Then Rollo's father explained the plan by which he was to learn to read. His sister Mary was to teach him. Mary was to call him to her every morning at nine o'clock, and teach him his letters for a quarter of an hour. She was to do the same at eleven, and at three, and at five. The rest of the time Rollo was to have for play. Mary was to take three or four of the letters at a time, and tell Rollo the names of them, and make them on the slate, and let him try to make them, and let him try to find them in books, until he should know them perfectly. She was to keep an account of every day, marking the days when, for any reasons, she did not hear him, and putting down, each day, the letters he learned that day, and as soon as he had learned all his letters she was to tell his father.

If he should at any time refuse to come when she called him, or come sullenly or in ill humor,—or if he disobeyed her, or made her any trouble, wilfully, she was to put the book away at once, and not teach

2

him any more that day, but at night tell his father.

When Rollo's father had thus explained the whole plan, he said,

"Now, Mary and Rollo, this is a hard task for both of you, I know. I hope you will both be patient and persevering,—and be kind to one another. Mary, you must remember that Rollo is a small boy, and cannot learn as fast as you might expect or wish,—you must be kind to him and patient. Be sure also to be punctual and regular in calling him at the exact hour. And Rollo you must be patient too and obedient, and you must remember that though it is hard work to learn to read, you will be very glad when you shall have learned. You will then enjoy a great many happy hours in sitting down by the fire in your little chair, and reading story books.

Soon after this Rollo went to bed thinking a great deal of his first lesson, which he was going to take the next day.

Do you not think now that it would have been better if Rollo's father had tried to make learning to read more amusing to his little boy? He might have got a book with letters and pictures too,—or he might have bought some blocks and cards with letters on them, and let Rollo learn by playing with them. That would have been more amusing. Do you think that would have been a better way? I think it would not. For if Rollo had begun to learn to read, expecting to find it play, he would have been disappointed and discouraged a great deal sooner. He might have looked at the pictures in his book, or played with the cards or the blocks, but that would not have taught him the letters on them. It was better that he should understand distinctly at the beginning that learning to read was hard work, and that he must attend to it *as a duty;* thus he would be prepared for it as it was, and find it more and more pleasant as he went along. But if he had expected that it would be play, he would only have been disappointed, and that would have made it harder, and made it take a great deal longer time.

Rollo liked reading very well for a day or two, but he soon became tired. He thought the quarter of an hour was very long, and that Mary always called him too soon. He was mistaken however in this, for Mary was always very exact and punctual. He found too that he got along very slowly. It was a good many days before he could say the first few letters, and he thought it would take a great while before he should have learned them all.

One pleasant morning, when he was digging with his little hoe, in the yard, Mary called him, and for a minute or two he had a great mind not to come. But then he recollected that if he did not, she would immediately put the book away and tell his father at night, so he threw down the hoe and ran. But it was very hard for him to do it.

In a few days one thing surprised both Mary and Rollo. It was that he learned the second four or five letters a great deal sooner than he did the first. They did not understand the reason of this. The third lesson was learned sooner still, and so on, the farther they went down the alphabet the faster Rollo learned.

One evening when Rollo had learned about half his letters, his father took him up in his lap and took a small round box out of his pocket with a pretty picture on

*a** *2**

the top. Besides the picture there were
three letters; they were these, A, B, C.
Rollo looked a moment at the picture, but
he was more pleased with the letters than
the picture. He was very much pleased
to see those letters,—the very letters
which he had learned, on the top of such
a pretty box.

"Oh there is A," said he, "and B, and
C, on the top of this pretty box. How
funny!"

Then his father opened the box and
poured out a great many beautiful round
cards into Rollo's lap. There were beautiful, painted pictures on one side and letters on the other. Rollo was most in-
terested in looking at the letters.

"Oh, father," said he, "what beautiful
cards! Why did you not buy them at
first, and let me learn my letters with
them?"

HOW ROLLO LEARNED TO READ. 19

"Because," said his father, "if I had bought them at first, when you did not know any of your letters, you would have not been pleased with any thing but the pictures, and rolling the cards about the floor. Or if I had given them to Mary to teach you your letters from them, then you would not have liked them any better than your book. But by letting you learn for a time from your book, till you know a good many letters, you can understand the cards, and you *notice* the letters on them, and when you play with them you will remember a great many letters on them and thus you will become more familiar with them."

"With what?" said Rollo.

"With the letters," said his father.

"What is *familiar with them*?" asked Rollo.

"Why you will know them better, and

remember them longer,—and you will
know them quicker when you see them
again in books. That is being familiar
with them. Do you not think you will
like this box of cards a great deal better
now, to play with, than before you knew
any letters?"

"Yes sir, I was very glad to see the
A B C on it."

After this Rollo played a great deal
with his cards, and though he did not learn
any new letters from them, they helped
him to become *familiar* with the letters
as fast as he learned them from his book.

The last part of the alphabet Rollo
learned very fast, and at length one evening Mary and Rollo came together to their
father, telling him with smiling faces that
he had learned them all.

Then Rollo's father gave him a long
lesson in reading little words;—he gave

him a great many columns, so many, that it would take a good many weeks to read them all. Mary was to hear him four times every day. Then he read the easy sentences over in the end of his book, and a good many others in another book, until at last he could read very well alone. It took a long time however to do all this reading. When he finished learning to read he was more than a year older than he was when he began. The stories in this book are for him to read, so that he may learn to read better. You can read them too. Farther on in this book I shall tell you more about Rollo.

In reading these stories Rollo found a great many words which he could not understand. He always asked some one what these words meant, for he wanted to understand what he read perfectly. His father advised him to read his story book aloud too, unless when it would disturb some one, because by reading aloud he would learn faster.

THE FIRST LESSONS IN LOOKING.

WHEN the baby was very little indeed and first began to open his eyes, his mother saw that the bright light of the windows dazzled them, and gave him pain; so she shut the blinds and put down the curtains.

When the baby was so very little, he did not know how to look about at the things which were around him. He had not learned to move his eyes steadily from one thing to another. He could not take hold of any thing, either, with his hands.

He did not know that his hands were made to take hold of things with. His mother held a handsome ivory ring before him, and endeavored to make him see it and take it. She put it in his hand, but he did not know how to hold it, and it dropped upon the floor.

The baby was very weak too. He could not walk nor sit up, nor even hold up his head. Unless his mother held his head for him it would drop down and hang upon his shoulder. Once she laid him down upon the bed and she went away a minute or two. While she was gone he rolled over on his face, and was so weak that he could not get back again. I do not think he knew how to try. His mother came back and lifted him up, or perhaps he would have been stifled.

One day his mother said, "Oh how many things I have got to teach my little child. I must teach him to look, and to hold up his head, and to take things in his hands, and I must do all these things while he is quite a little baby."

She thought she would first teach him *to look*. So she let in a little light and when he was quiet and still, she held him so that he could see it. But he did not seem to notice it, and pretty soon he went to sleep.

The next day she tried it again; and again on the following day, and soon she found that he would look very steadily at the white curtain, or at the place where the sun shone upon the wall. She did not yet try to make him look at *little things*, for she knew she could not hope to make him see little things till he had learned to notice something large and bright.

When Samuel was lying in his mother's lap, looking steadily at something, she was always careful not to move him, or to make any noise, or to do any thing which would distract his attention.   She knew that children were always puzzled with having two things to think of at a time, and she was afraid that if while he was thinking of the light and trying to look at it, he should hear voices around him, he would stop thinking of the light, and begin to wonder what that noise could be.

In about a week, Samuel had learned his lesson very well.   He could look pretty steadily at a large bright spot when it was still.   Then his mother thought she would try to teach him to look at something smaller.   She therefore asked his father to buy her a large bright orange, and one day when he was lying quietly in her lap, she held it up be-

b   3

fore him. But he would not notice it;
he seemed to be looking at the window
beyond.

Then his mother turned her chair gently round, and sat with her back towards
the window so that he could not see the
window and then he looked at the orange.
Presently she moved the orange slowly,—
very slowly,—backwards and forwards, to
teach him to follow it with his eyes.
Thus the baby took his first lessons in
looking.

TICK,—TICK,—TICK.

ONE morning I was going to take a
journey. I was going in the stage. I
expected that the sleigh bells would come
jingling up to the door for me at seven

o'clock. So I thought that if I wished to be ready, I must get up at *six*.

I went into my little room where I was to sleep. There was a clock on the wall, by the side of my bed. It said tick,—tick,—tick. "I am glad," said I to myself, "for now I can see what o'clock it is." So I put my lamp down on the floor, and put my spectacles behind my pillow, and then laid down and went to sleep.

By and by I woke and thought I heard a little noise. I listened. It was the clock, saying tick,—tick,—tick; and I said to myself, "I wonder what o'clock it is?" So I sat up and took my spectacles from behind my pillow and put them on my nose, and looked up at the clock. The lamp which was on the floor shone upon the clock so that I could see, and I saw that it was only *three* o'clock, and I said, "Oh it is only three o'clock. It is not time

for me to get up yet." So I took my
spectacles off of my nose, and put them
behind my pillow and laid me down again.
The clock kept saying tick,—tick,—tick.

Pretty soon I went to sleep and I slept
an hour. Then I awoke and said to myself, " I wonder what o'clock it is ?" So I
sat up and took my spectacles from behind my pillow, and put them on my
nose, and looked up at the clock. The
lamp which was upon the floor shone
upon the clock, so that I could see, and I
saw that it was only *four* o'clock, and I
said, " Oh, it is only four o'clock; it is
not time for me to get up yet." So I
took my spectacles off of my nose, and
put them behind my pillow, and laid me
down again. The clock kept saying all
the while, tick,—tick,—tick.

Pretty soon, I went to sleep, and slept
some time. Then I woke and said to

myself, "I wonder what o'clock it is?"
So I sat up, and took my spectacles from
behind my pillow, and put them on my
nose, and looked up at the clock. The
lamp which was upon the floor shone
upon the clock, so that I could see, and I
saw that it was only *five* o'clock, and I
said, "Oh, it is only five o'clock. It is not
time for me to get up yet." So I took
my spectacles off of my nose, and put
them behind my pillow, and laid me down
again. The clock kept saying all the
while, tick,—tick,—tick.

Pretty soon I went to sleep, and slept
some time. When I woke, I said to myself, "I wonder what o'clock it is?" So
I sat up and took my spectacles from behind my pillow, and put them on my
nose, and looked up at the clock. The
lamp which was upon the floor shone
upon the clock so that I could see, and I

3*

saw that it was *six* o'clock. Then I said *now* it is time for me to get up. So I jumped up and dressed me, and looked out of the window, and there was a beautiful, bright star shining in the sky. The star was up before me.

When I was ready I opened the door to go out; but the clock still kept saying tick,—tick,—tick. I wondered what made the clock keep going so all the night and all the day, and I went back and opened the door to see. And what do you think I found? Why I found a great heavy weight hung to a string, and the string was fastened to some of the little wheels up in the clock. The weight kept pulling down and pulling down all the time, slowly, and it pulled the string down slowly, and the string made the wheels go round, and the wheels made the hands go, and some of the little wheels made that noise I heard,—tick—tick—tick.

What do you think happens when the weights which make the clock go get down, down, to the very bottom of the clock? Why then they have to wind them up to the top again, and they begin anew.

JONAS.

ONE fine summer evening a gentleman came riding down a hill in a country covered with pleasant farm houses, green fields, and little groups of trees. He had a small boy in the waggon with him.

There was a brook at the bottom of the hill. A bridge was built over the brook, and the road passed over the bridge. The horse and waggon with the gentleman and his boy in it, went swiftly over the bridge and up the hill, but just as they began to ascend, one of the *traces* broke.

One of the *traces*? What is a trace? Do you know, my boy? The traces are those long stout straps of leather which pass along the sides of the horse, and are fastened to the waggon. The horse draws a waggon, or a chaise, by means of the traces. Therefore they are always made very strong. You can see a picture of some traces in "Rollo learning to Talk," a book about as large this, at the story of a Goat for a Horse. The next time you take a ride, I advise you to look at the traces on the horse, and see how strong they are. See too how they are fastened to the horse and how they are fastened to the chaise.

If one of the traces should give way, that is, should break, in going up a hill, what do you think would be the consequence? Why the waggon would go back, partly held by the other trace. That was the way with this waggon; it went back, the horse was frightened, the gentleman jumped out, the boy called out, " whoa,—*whoa*,—WHOA."

It did not do any good. Boys had better be still when there is any difficulty.

The waggon backed until, just as it was going off the bank, a boy ran up and put a stone behind the wheel. That stopped it.

This was not the boy who was in the waggon. It was another boy. The gentleman had not seen him before. He had on light colored clothes, a patched jacket, and an old straw hat, one side of the brim was almost worn out with catching butterflies; the knees of his trowsers were stained with the grass. The gentleman looked at him a minute, and said " thank

you, my boy." Then he began to look at
the harness. When the gentleman had
examined the traces he found that the
leather was not broken; it was only the
tongue of a buckle by which the trace
was fastened that was gone; for the harness was new, and the waggon was a
handsome one.

"I wish I had a piece of twine to fast-
en it with, till we get home," said he to
his son, as he felt in his pockets. He
then looked round to see where the little
fellow was who had *trigged* the wheel.
Do you know what I mean by trigging
the wheel? The boy was sitting on the
trunk of a tree, by the side of the road,
and as the gentleman turned round to see
him, he was just pulling out a long piece
of twine from his pocket.

"Here is a string, sir," said he; and he
got up and came to the gentleman. He -

seemed tired however, for he went back
and sat down again immediately.

"I thank you," said he, "but I am
afraid it is not strong enough."

"You can double and twist it," said
the boy.

They twisted the string, and then
doubled it and twisted it again, and so
tied the harness. The gentleman and
his son then got into the waggon again,
and were going to ride up the hill. The
gentleman hesitated a moment whether
he ought to offer to pay the boy for his
string or not. Do you think he ought
to?

"I *would* pay him," whispered his little son; "he looks like a poor boy."

"Yes," replied his father, "but perhaps
he would make a bad use of the money.
Perhaps his father and mother would not
like to have him have any money."

"Why cannot you ask him?"

The gentleman then turned to the boy who was still sitting on the log, and said,

"What is your name my little fellow?"

"Jonas."

"Where do you live?"

"Sir?"

"Where do you live?"

The boy hesitated a moment as if he did not understand him. Then he said,

"I don't know sir:—I don't live any where."

The little boy in the waggon laughed.

"Don't know where you live?" said the gentleman. "Well what are you doing out here?"

"I have been catching butterflies."

"Where did you come from?"

"I don't know sir.—I came from the city."

"The city! What city?"

"I don't know sir,—the city back there. I don't know what the name of it is."

Jonas sitting on a log.

"Do you live in the city?"

"No sir, I am not going to live there any more?"

"Do your father and mother live there?"

"My father is dead; and I have not got any mother."

"What has become of your mother?"

"I never had any, sir."

The gentleman smiled a moment when he heard this answer, and then he looked serious and concerned and paused a moment. He seemed not to know what to do.

"But Jonas," said he again, "you say you do not live any where; where do you get your food and sleep?"

"Sir!"

"Where do you sleep at night?"

"I slept in Mr. Williams' shed last night."

"And where do you expect to sleep to night?"

"I don't know sir."

"Where did you get your breakfast this morning?"

"A man gave me some."

"And where did you get your dinner?"

"I have not had any dinner sir."

"No dinner!—I should think you would be too tired and hungry to chase butter-flies, without any dinner."

"I was too tired, and so I stopped."

The gentleman after talking with the boy a little longer concluded to take him into his waggon, and carry him home.

"Jump up behind into my waggon, Jonas," said he, "and I will give you some supper."

So Jonas jumped up behind and rode home with them. You will hear more about him hereafter, for who do you think this gentleman was? Why it was Rollo's father, and the boy who was riding with him was Rollo himself. Jonas lived with Rollo a long time and became a very industrious, useful boy. He used to take care of Rollo, and play with him.

A LITTLE LETTER.

THIS is a letter written to a little boy about as large as you. James is the name of the boy. James' uncle wrote it.

The letter.

"Dear James,

Do you want me to write you a little letter about a robin? I think you do. Well; I will write it. Now I will begin. A robin is a bird. A robin has two wings and two legs; he flies in

*b** 4*

the air; it is his wings make him go.
When he comes down to the ground, he
hops along on his two legs. When he
sees a worm he picks it up with his bill.
Do you know what his *bill* is? It is a
mouth. Then he picks it up just as the
hen does, and eats it. Now for the story.

Near the house where I live, there is a
field; and in the field there is a tree. I
was walking in the field, and went near
the tree; as I went near it, a bird darted
out of the tree, and sung out very loud;
it made me start. When I saw it was a
bird, I looked among the leaves and
branches of the tree, and found there a
pretty robin's nest, and three eggs. Only
think, a beautiful nest, with three eggs. I
looked at them for a minute, and then
went away and left them there. The
next day, I walked down to the tree
again, to see the nest and the pretty eggs.

I pulled away the leaves, but the nest was not there. I stooped down on the ground, looked into the grass, and there I saw the robin. The poor robin was dead, the nest was torn in pieces, and the eggs were broken. I would send you one of the eggs, but it is broken so much, that I think it will not do. When the little robin was alive, he sung pleasantly, he made him a nest, and had some eggs; but now the robin is dead, the nest is torn in pieces, and the eggs are broken. Poor robin; poor robin.

I have written this story of the robin for little James. I am very sorry that any boy should kill the poor robin and spoil its nest.

This is from your affectionate,

Uncle."

ROLLO'S DREAM.

ONE day Rollo's mother wanted him
to do some errands for her. He went on
one, reluctantly, but when she gave him
another he murmured aloud. "Oh," said
he, "I wish I did not have so many errands to do. What a hard life I lead!"

This gave his mother pain, and he saw
it. When he got back from this errand
she told him there was nothing more for
him to do. Rollo went and stood at the
door a few minutes to see if there were
any boys out there. But there were none,
so he took a story-book in his hand and
went down into the garden, and took his
seat in the little arbor which his father had
made for him, and began to read.

The arbor reminded him of his parents'
kindness, and this made him feel unhappy

And here you see Rollo fast asleep.—*Page* 46.

to think of his unwillingness to help his mother. These thoughts troubled him, and so he could not attend to his book. Presently he got lost in a reverie,—his book dropped over upon his lap. His head gradually sunk down,—and here you see Rollo fast asleep.

While he slept, he dreamed. Rollo dreamed that he lived in a small house, a great many miles away, and that his mother was there alone with him. She asked him one day to go and get a pail of water. "Oh," said he, "I wish I did not have so much water to bring,—what a hard life I lead!"

He dreamed that just then he saw a cat lying down in the sun by the door. She seemed to have nothing to do. "Oh," thought Rollo, "how I wish I were a cat. It would be such a *fine thing* to be a cat."

No sooner had he said this than he felt

some how or other a strong desire to get down on his hands and knees,—he found himself growing smaller and smaller,—his fingers became sharp claws, and in short Rollo dreamed that he was turning into a cat.

He walked about, a minute or two, stretched himself, mewed and purred to ascertain that he was really a cat, and then laid down again in the sun to go to sleep. As he shut his eyes he said to himself, purring, "How glad I am that I have no more water to bring! What a fine thing it is to be a cat!"

Pretty soon he waked up and was hungry. His first thought was to go to his mother as usual, for some bread and butter. He went in and looked piteously up into his mother's face, and mewed. She did not mind him. He mewed louder. She paid no attention. Then he went to making a louder noise, as cats can, when necessary. His mother went and opened the door, and took the brush and drove him out, saying as he went, "*scat*."

Rollo then thought he must go and catch some mice or starve. So he went down cellar and posted himself before a little hole in the wall. He waited here an hour, and at length a little mouse peeped out. Rollo darted his paw out at him, but he missed him, and the mouse drew back into his hole where he was safe. Rollo waited many hours longer, but no mouse came. "This is worse than bringing water," thought he. "I wish I *could* get something to eat. What a hard life I lead!"

Just then he heard, that is, he dreamed he heard, a loud noise, moo-o-o, in the yard. He scampered up, hungry as he was, to see what was the matter. It was

c 5

the cow lowing to be milked. She looked
full and large, as if she had had as much
as she could eat.

"In the green fields all day," thought
hungry Rollo, "with nothing to do but
eat and drink and then lie down under
the trees. Oh how I wish I were a cow!"

He had no sooner said these words
than he found himself growing very large.
He felt something coming out of his fore-
head,—he put his paw up, though with
difficulty for his paw was growing into a
large stiff leg, and he found that horns
were coming. By the time his leg was
down again, it was changed entirely, and
had a hoof at the end. He was becoming
a cow. He lashed his sides with his tail,
and walked about eating the grass in the
yard, till he had satisfied his hunger, and
then he said to himself; "How much
better this is than watching for mice all

day in a dark cellar! Oh it is a fine thing to be a cow."

After milking, they led Rollo into the barn, put a halter round his neck and tied him in a dark, unpleasant stall. "Have I got to stay tied up here till morning?" thought Rollo. It was even so.

The next morning they drove him off to pasture. The boy beat him with a stick on the way, but he was so great and clumsy that he could neither escape nor defend himself. In the field, the flies bit and stung him, and though he could brush off some of them with his tail, yet the largest and worst of them always seemed to get upon places he could not reach. At night when he was coming home, some boys set a dog upon him and worried him till he was weary of his life. "Ah," said he, "it is a terrible thing to be a cow,—what a hard life I lead!"

Just then the dog became tired of barking at him, and trotted away. "Oh said Rollo, "if I was only a dog. A dog can defend himself. Then a dog has plenty to eat and nothing to do. What a fine thing it would be to be a dog!" No sooner said than done. Rollo began to grow slender and small, his horns dropped off,—his hoofs turned back into claws again, his back became sleek and shining, and he found himself a beautiful black dog, with hanging ears and a curled tail, and an elegant brass collar about his neck.

Rollo ran about the streets very happily for half an hour, and then went home. The dream seemed to change its scene here, and Rollo found himself in a beautiful yard belonging to the house where his master lived. He went home hungry, and they gave him a bone to eat. "What," said Rollo to himself, "nothing but a bone!" He gnawed it for a while, thinking however that it was rather hard fare, and then began to think of going to bed. There was no bed for him however; for his master came and took hold of his collar, and led him along towards a post in the yard, where he chained him, and throwing his bone down by his side, left him to watch for the thieves.

Rollo had a bad night. 'Tis true no thieves came, but he was all the time afraid they would come, and at every little noise he woke up and growled. Thus disturbed, and chilled by the cool air of the night, he passed his hours restlessly and miserably. "Ah!" said he, "dogs do not have so pleasant a life as I supposed. What a hard way this is to get a living!"

At this moment he heard a great many persons coming along; he started up and

5*

barked, for it was very early, though beginning to be light. A number of men were leading a huge animal along. It was an elephant. They were taking him into town for a show, and they came in early, so that nobody should see him without paying.

"That's the life for me," said Rollo. "What a gentleman of an animal the elephant is; he has a dozen men to wait upon him. Hah! Old Longnose, what a happy fellow you must be. Oh if I was only an elephant!"

As soon as he had said this he could feel his nose lengthening into a slender trunk,—his body swelled out to a great size,—his feet grew large, and his black shining skin turned into a coarse, rough, grey hide,—and he found himself walking along the road, with a man on his head.

He arrived at the great stable where he

was to be exhibited, thinking that it was an admirable thing to be an elephant. They gave him something to eat, and soon the men and boys came in to see him. For half an hour, he had a fine time, walking around, carrying boys about on his tusks,—taking his keeper's head into his mouth,—picking up nuts and pieces of gingerbread with the finger and thumb at the end of his proboscis,—laying down and rising again at the keeper's command. Pretty soon, however, he got tired, and when the keeper ordered him to lay down, he concluded that he would not get up again. But the keeper taught him by blows that he was not his own master, if he was a gentleman. New troops of starers kept coming in, and Rollo got tired out completely with going over and over again the same evolutions. He could hardly stand at last, and when they left him for the night and he lay down to try to rest, and he reflected that it must be just so to-morrow, and the next day, and so on as long as he lived, he was almost in despair. "Oh!" said he, "how foolish I was to wish to be an elephant! I had rather be any thing else. What a hard life I lead!"

"And then such a window as this to look out of, after my hard day's work;" said he, as he turned his eye upward towards a little square hole in the stable wall. "What a window for an elephant's residence!"

As he looked out this hole, his eye rested upon a green tree growing in a garden behind the wall. A bird was perched upon a branch, singing an evening song.

"Ah, you little bird, what a happy time you must have there,—free as air, and full of happiness. You find plenty to eat, you have your own pleasant home upon a lofty tree, out of the reach of any danger. You go where you please with your swift wings. Oh if I only had wings, how easily I could escape from all my troubles."

As he said this his long proboscis which was lying over his leg as he was reclining upon the stable floor, began to straiten out and stiffen,—turning into a huge bill, —feathers began to come out all over him,—his immense body dwindled down to the size of an ox, then to that of a sheep, and finally he became smaller than a dove. Beautiful wings covered his sides. He hopped along upon the floor, and finding that he was really a bird, he leaped up and flew out of the window,—away from the ugly stable forever.

He spent a pleasant night among the trees, and early the next morning was singing blithely upon a branch. A man came into the field with something in his hand. Rollo looked at him, happy to think that no man could catch him or hurt him, now that he had such a pair of wings. In a minute the man held up the thing he had in his hands and pointed at him. Rollo had just time to see that it was a gun, and to stretch his wings in terrible fear, when,—*flash*,—BANG,—went the gun, and down came the poor bird to the ground, with his wing and leg torn away, and a dozen leaden shot lodged in his red breast,—for he was a Robin. The terror and pain waked him up, and he found himself sitting in his arbor, with his book on the ground, where it had fallen from his hand. He got up and went to the house, thinking that a discontented mind would find trouble enough in any situation, and that a boy with kind parents, a pleasant home, and plenty of food and clothing, ought not to complain of his lot, even if he was called upon sometimes to help his mother.

THE COLD MORNING.

ONE pleasant morning in the fall of the year, little Charles, who had been sleeping on the trundle-bed in his mother's chamber, waked up and opened his eyes. He looked around him, and saw that his father was dressing himself.

"Father," said he, "may I get up too?"

"It is pretty cold this morning, can you bear the cold long enough to dress yourself?"

"But, father, I need not stay here; I can take up my clothes and run down into the parlor, and dress me there by the fire."

"No, it is not proper for any body to go to the parlor till they are dressed. Besides, perhaps the fire is not built yet."

By this time, Charles' nose had become pretty cold; so he said, "Well, I believe I will wait;" and he drew his head under the bedclothes again.

In a few minutes he became warm again, and thought that it would not be very cold if he should get up, and that if it was, he should not mind it. He looked out a second time and said,

"Father, do you think I should have time to dress me before you get ready to go down stairs?"

"I think you will, if you are quick."

"Do you think I could help you any in building the fire?"

"Yes, you might hand me the wood,

and carry out the ashes, and after the fire is built, you might sweep up the hearth."

"Then I will get up," said Charles, and he sprang out of bed, and began to dress himself.

In a few minutes, however, he began to be cold, and to shiver, and his fingers grew numb, and he began to wish he had waited a little longer. At last he stopped dressing himself.

"Father," said he, "it is colder than I thought it was. I have a great mind to get into bed again."

"Well," said his father, "you can do as you please, but how far have you got, in dressing yourself?"

"I am about half dressed."

"Then it will take you about as long to undress again as it would to finish dressing, and be ready to go down."

6

Charles stood a moment shivering and thinking.

"So it will," said he, "I wish I had not put on my jacket."

After a moment's pause, he concluded to finish dressing, and he went on resolutely through it, and just as his father opened the door, he took hold of his hand, saying that he was ready.

"Father," said he, as they were going down stairs, "I think that when any body means to do any thing, he ought to think of all the difficulties before he begins, and then go through it quickly without stop ping."

"Why?" said his father.

"Because I grew colder while I was standing still, not knowing what to do. than all the time while I was dressing me. And now I shall be very cold before we get the fire built.   Father, I don't see what makes it cold. I wish it was always warm as it is in summer."

"While we are building the fire, I will explain it to you," said his father. So they went down stairs.

When Rollo read this story he said he was sorry it left off without telling why it is colder in the winter than in the summer, because he thought he should like to know. So at breakfast that morning, he asked his father to explain it to him. "Yes," said his father, "I will explain it to you. It is because in the winter the sun moves through such a part of the sky that he does not shine so well upon the part of the world which we live in, as he does in the summer."

Rollo listened attentively to what his father said, but he thought he did not understand it very well. So he said he meant always to dress himself quick in the cold morning, and not keep beginning and leaving off as Charles did.

HOW TO READ RIGHT.

I WISH all the boys and girls who may read this book to learn by it to read right, and now I shall tell you how to read right. But first I must explain some things to you about the way in which books are printed. What I am going to tell you now, is what Rollo's father explained to him, after he had learned to read in easy reading, and had learned all the stops,— the comma, and the period, and the interrogation mark, and all the stops. I shall explain them to you by the help of a story, which I am going to put in here. I shall stop telling the story every few minutes to explain some things about the way of printing it. Here is the beginning of the story.

Once there was a man who thought he would go up upon a mountain.

That is the beginning of the story ; but I wish to stop a moment to ask you to look at the letters which it is printed with, and see whether they are as large as the reading before it. Is it printed in just as large letters, or larger, or smaller ? Yes, it is smaller. I am going to have all the story printed in smaller print. The reason is because the principal thing I wish to do now, is to explain to you how to read, and I only wish for the story to help me,—so I put it in smaller print, or as they generally call it smaller *type*. It is very often so in books. One part is print-ed in larger, and the other part in smaller

c *   6*

type. The most important is in large
type. The least important is in small
type. If you will ask your father or mother, or your brother or sister if you have
one old enough, they will show you books
with large and small print in them. Whenever you see any thing printed in smaller
print than the rest of the book, you ought
not to read right on without thinking any-
thing of it;—but you ought to pause a
minute, and observe it, and think what
the reason is. Now I will begin my story
again, in small print.

Once there was a man who thought he would go up upon
a mountain; so he rode along on his horse till he came as
near to the mountain as he could, in the road,—and then he
turned off into the woods and rode on until he came to the
foot of the mountain. He could ride no farther; so he tied
his horse to a tree.

Then he began to walk up the mountain.

Do you see that when we come to the
word *tree*, just above there, that we leave

off printing in that line. There is a period, and then the rest of the line has nothing in it. It is blank, as they call it, that is white, all white paper. The next part of the story begins in the next line. The next part of the story is, these words, "Then he began," and that is printed in the next line. And if you look at it, you will see that it is not exactly at the beginning of the line. The word "Then" is not printed as near the side of the page as the other lines above it are. There is a little space left blank. Do you see the little space left blank before the "Then?" Now what do you suppose is the reason why we left off in the middle of the line and began again in the next line, leaving a little blank space? Why it is because I had finished telling you all about the man's *coming to* the mountain, and was now going to tell you about his *going up* the mountain, and so I thought it would be best to leave of for that line, and begin again in the next. Should you like to know what such a place is called? It is called a new paragraph. A new paragraph is made whenever we come to any new part of the story. If you look back over the leaves of this book you will find a great many new paragraphs on all the pages. If any person says any thing in the story, we put what he says in a paragraph by itself. See if you can find some new paragraphs.

Now, when you come to any new paragraph in your reading, you ought not to read right forward without stopping or noticing it at all. You should pause a little when one paragraph ends, and then begin again when the new paragraph begins, so that those who hear you read, and who are not looking over, may know by the sound of your voice, that you have come to a new paragraph.

Now I will go on with the story, again, beginning at the new paragraph.

Then he began to walk up. He scrambled through the bushes for some time, and at last came out into a smooth, but muddy path. Here, however, he was in no little difficulty, for the path was so slippery that notwithstanding all he could do, he seemed rather to be sliding *down*, than climbing up.

Here we come to the end of another paragraph. And I wish you to look at the word " *down*" in the last line. Do you see any thing strange about it? Is it printed like the other words?

Once I asked some children to look at a word printed so, and to tell me what the difference was between it and other words. One said it looked fainter. Another said it looked smaller. A third said it was not printed with good ink. But the true explanation is, the letters of the word are slanting. That is all. It makes the word look a little fainter.

You will see that the letters are different by looking first at the d in "sliding," which comes before "*down*," and then looking at the *d* in "*down*." The d in "sliding" is straight. The *d* in "*down*" is slanting; all the other letters in *down* are slanting. Do you know what this kind of printing is called? It is called Italic.

The word "*down*" in the story is printed in Italics. The reason why it is printed in Italics is because I wanted you to notice it particularly. It is remarkable that while the man was trying to get *up*, he should instead of that slide *down*. So I had the word printed differently, that you might notice it particularly. Whenever you are reading and come to any word

printed in Italics you must notice it, and
speak it very distinctly, for it is an important
word.

Look back in this book and see if you
can find some words printed in Italics.
When you find one, read the sentence it
is in aloud, and speak the word which is
in Italics very plain and distinct, and see
if you do not understand the sentence
better.

You must always read such words very
distinctly in all books except the Bible.
In the Bible, the words are put in Italics
for a different reason, which I cannot explain
to you now. Now I will go on with
the story.

He at last got over this slippery part of the path, and
then came to a place where it was very rocky. Trees and
bushes hung over his head, and grew thick all around him,
and he began to be afraid that he might meet some wild
beast. Presently he looked through the bushes and saw at
a distance among the rocks some large black thing, and he

thought it was a bear. He was very much frightened and began to scream out as loud as he could, HELP, HELP, HELP.

Do you notice any thing remarkable in those three last words? Are they printed like the other words? Are they printed in Italics? How do they differ from common printing? Can you tell? Do you often see words printed so?

They are printed in Capitals. Capitals are letters shaped differently from other letters. They are generally larger than other letters, but not always. These words are printed in capitals, because they are very important indeed. The man cried Help, Help, Help, very loud. So we print them in Capitals. If a word is very important, we generally print it in Italics, but if it is *very* important *indeed*, we print it in Capitals. When you come to a word printed in Capitals, you must generally read it very plain and distinctly indeed. I should like to have you look back to the story of Jonas, and see how the words are printed where the boy said, "Whoa." Can you tell the reason why they are printed so? and can you read them right? But let us go on with the story.

At the same time that he shouted for help so loud, he grasped hold of a tree close by, and began to climb it, by the branches, to get out of the bear's way. When he got up a little way he could see over the bushes to the very place where the bear was; he looked there, and saw — what do you think it was?

You see a straight mark printed after "saw." Do you see it? What do you suppose it is? It is what they call a *dash*. The reason why I put the dash there, is that I was going to tell you what the man saw, but I suddenly stopped, and asked you what you thought it was. When we

d   7

suddenly stop in saying any thing, and begin to say something else, we put in a *dash*. So we use a dash in some other ways. You ought to stop a little when you come to a dash, thus; " He looked there and saw — what do you think it was ?" Dashes are generally put in, when we want you to stop a little in your reading. Now for the story again.

He looked, and saw — what do you think it was ? Why it was nothing but an old, black log ! !

Do you see two characters at the end of that sentence ? They are notes of exclamation. When two of them are put together they mean that what comes before them is very extraordinary and surprising. Should not you think it was very extraordinary and surprising for a man to think he saw a bear, and be frightened and shout help, and climb up into a tree, and find, after all, that it was nothing but a great, black log? It is surprising, and when you read it, you must read it as if you thought it was very surprising, so; "What do you think it was? Why it was nothing but an old, black log!!" You can get your father or mother to show you how to read it, if you do not know.

It was nothing but an old, black log, lying against the rocks. The man felt ashamed. He clambered down, and went to look at the log which had frightened him so. It was as black as a coal.* The man laughed to think that he should have supposed *that* to be a bear.

Do you see after the word *coal*, in the last line but one, a little star. Do you know what that star is for? It is to make you look down to the bottom of the page, and there you will find something more about the black wood. When you come

* It was burnt black by a fire, which somebody had built there a great while before.

to any little star then, when you are reading, you must look down to the bottom
of the page, and there you will find another little star, with something printed
after it.   That which is printed thus at the
bottom of a page is called a *note*.

Other characters besides stars are made
for notes.   These are some of the characters ; § ¶ † ‡.   There are not many notes
in this book.   Perhaps you will find some
by and by.

This is all that I have to tell you now
about reading.   But now I will put in the
whole story about the man going up the
mountain, and you may see if you can
read it all right, and see too if you remember all that I have explained.

CLIMBING UP A MOUNTAIN.

Once there was a man who thought he would go up upon a mountain; so he rode along upon his horse till he came as near the mountain as he could, and then he turned off into the woods and rode on until he came to the foot of the mountain. He could ride no farther; so he tied his horse to a tree.

Then he began to walk up. He scrambled through the bushes for some time, and at last came out into a smooth but muddy path. Here, however, he was in no little difficulty, for the path was so slippery that notwithstanding all he could do, he seemed rather to be sliding *down* than climbing *up*.

He at last got over this slippery part of the path, and then came to a place

where it was very rocky. Trees and
bushes hung over his head, and grew thick,
all around him, and he began to be afraid
that he might meet with some wild beast.
Presently he looked through the bushes,
and saw at a distance among the rocks,
some large, black thing, and he thought it
was a bear. He was very much frightened, and began to scream out as loud as
he could, HELP, HELP, HELP.

At the same time that he shouted for
help so loud, he grasped hold of a tree
close by, and began to climb it, by the
branches, to get out of the bear's way.
When he got up a little way he could see
over the bushes to the very place where
the bear was ; he looked there and saw,
— what do you think it was? Why it
was nothing but *an old, black log!!* An
old black log, lying against the rocks. The
man felt ashamed. He clambered down

and went to look at the log which had frightened him so. It was as black as a coal.* The man laughed to think that he should have supposed *that* to be a bear.

He determined not to be so foolish another time, and then he went along climbing up the mountain. It was steep and rocky, and there were bushes and trees each side of the path. He had to stop often to take breath and rest himself. At last he reached the top, and could see a great many miles all around. He could see woods and farms and towns and rivers away down, down, very far below him.

After a while he came down the mountain. He walked very carefully, so as not to fall. When he came to where the old black log was, he looked at it and laughed.

* It was burnt black by a fire which somebody had built there a great while before.

ROLLO GETTING READY
FOR HIS FATHER.

ONE day little Rollo was sitting by the fire on his green cricket. His mother was sewing at her work-table.

"Mother," said Rollo, "when do you think father will come home?"

His mother said, "I think he will come home pretty soon."

"Then," said Rollo, "I think I had better get a chair for him."

So he went and took hold of the great rocking-chair, to pull it to the fire for his father; but it was so heavy that it would not come. So Rollo began to cry.

His mother looked up and said, "Rollo, what is the matter?"

Rollo said, "This rocking-chair will not come."

It was so heavy it would not come.

"Where do you want to carry it?"

"I want it to be by the fire, so that my father can sit in it when he comes home," said Rollo.

"Why do you want your father to have it?"

"Because;" said he. He did not know exactly how to tell the reason, and so he only said "Because."

"It is because you wish to please him and to save him trouble, is it not?"

"Yes mother," said Rollo.

"Well, do you not think it displeases me and gives me trouble to have you cry, and make me get up and come and move the chair for you?"

Rollo knew it did, but he did not answer.

Then his mother said, "What good does it do to displease *me* and make *me* trouble, for the sake of pleasing *father* and saving *him* trouble ?"

Rollo could not answer this question ; so he kept swinging and rocking, back and forth, on the chair. His mother went on with her work.

By and by he said, "Well, I can get my father's slippers for him."

So he went to the little closet by the side of the fire, and took out the slippers, and put them down in the corner, and then when his father came in, he ran to the door to meet him, and he said,

"Father, father, I could not move up your chair, but there are your slippers all ready."

THE WAY TO OBEY.

WHEN Rollo was about five years old, his mother one evening took him up in her lap, and said,

"Well Rollo, it is about time for you to go to bed."

"Oh mamma," said Rollo, "*must* I go now?"

"Did you know," said his mother, "that it is wrong for you to say that?"

"Why, mother," said Rollo, surprised.

"When I think it is time for you to go to bed, it is wrong for you to say or do any thing which shows that you are not willing to go."

"Why mother?"

"Because that makes it more unpleasant for you to go, and more unpleasant for me to send you. Now whenever I think that it is time for you to go, it is my duty to send you, and it is your duty to go, and we never ought to do any thing to make our duty unpleasant.

Rollo then said nothing. He sat still a few minutes thinking.

8

"Do you understand it?" said his mother.

"Yes mother;" said Rollo.

"Suppose now any mother should say to her boy, 'Come my boy, it is time for you to go to bed;' and the boy should say, 'I wont go.' Would that be right or wrong?"

"Oh very wrong," said Rollo.

"Suppose he should begin to cry, and say he did not want to go?"

"That would be very wrong too," said Rollo.

"Suppose he should begin to beg a little, and say, 'I don't want to go *now;* I should think you might let me set up a little longer.' What should you think of that?"

"It would be wrong."

"Suppose he should look up into his mother's face sorrowfully, and say, '*Must* I go now, mother.'"

"Wrong,"—said Rollo, faintly.

"Suppose he should not say a word, but look cross and ill-humored, and throw away his playthings in a pet, and walk by the side of his mother reluctantly and slowly. What should you think of that?"

"I think it would be wrong."

"Suppose he should look pleasantly, and say 'Well mother,' and come pleasantly to take her hand, and bid the persons in the room good night, and walk off cheerfully."

"That would be right;" said Rollo.

"Yes," said his mother, "and always, when a child is told to do any thing, whether it is pleasant to do or not, he ought to obey at once, and cheerfully."

ROLLO'S BREAKFAST.

ROLLO was sitting one morning by the fire-side, before breakfast, reading in a little blue covered hymn-book. Presently Mary brought in the breakfast; and Rollo was glad, and jumped up from his little *low* chair at the fire, and went and brought his *high* chair, and put it at his place at the table.

When they were all ready, they stood still, while Rollo's father said in a slow and serious manner, "Almighty God, we thank thee that thou hast again spread this table for us and prepared this food. Help us now to receive it thankfully, and may it strengthen us to obey thy commands this day; we ask it for Christ's sake." Then they sat down.

Rollo knew that this was called asking

a blessing, and he had always been taught to be very still and very attentive while it was done. He did not know however exactly what it was for, and he thought he would now ask his father.

His father told him that it was to thank God for their breakfast.

Rollo asked his father whether God gave them their breakfast.

"Yes," said his father, "God causes our breakfast to be brought to us from many distant places."

"Where do the knives and forks come from?" said Rollo.

"They come from England. The men dig up the iron out of the ground to make the blades, and take horn and make the handles, and then roll them up in a paper and put them in a ship. The ship brings them across the ocean more than a thousand miles to Boston. Then the wag-

d *   8*

goner puts them in his waggon and brings them over the hills and valleys away to this town where we live,—all that little Rollo may have a knife and fork to eat his breakfast."

"Where do the plates come from?"

"They come from England. The men find a bank of white clay, and they mix up some of it with water, until it is like dough. Then they make it into the shape of plates, and cups, and saucers, and paint them blue; and put them into a large hot oven and bake them hard. When they are cooled, they pack them up in a sort of a basket large and square; and put straw and hay between them, so that they need not break. And so they bring them over the waves, and over the hills, away to the town we live in, so that little Rollo may have a plate when he eats his breakfast."

"Where does the coffee come from?"

"It comes from Cuba. The negroes plant a tree and take good care of it while it grows, until there are a great many kernels of coffee upon it. They gather them when they are ripe, and sew them up in a bag, and send them all the way over the sea, and over the land, across the rivers, and mountains and rocks. When they come here, Mary burns them brown and grinds them in the mill, and heats the water, all that little Rollo may have some coffee to drink for breakfast."

"Where does the bread come from?"

"When the summer begins, the little green blades of wheat grow up out of the ground, in the farmer's fields. God waters it with showers, and warms it with the sun, so that it grows and grows and grows, till it is higher than Rollo's head. Then the little grains of wheat grow in the top of it, and when they are ripe, the farmer cuts them down, and pounds them out with a great heavy flail, and puts them in a bag and sends them to mill. At the mill they are ground between two great stones, into fine white flour, and the baker mixes the flour and water; and makes the dough, and bakes it in his great hot oven, all that little Rollo may have some bread for breakfast."

"Well, but father," said Rollo, "how does God give us our breakfast then?"

His father said, "Why, it is God who made the iron in the ground for the knives, and the clay for the plates and cups. He brings the summer and the sun. He makes the wheat sprout up and grow, and brings the showers of rain. He takes care too of all the men who shape the cups and make the knives, and gather the coffee, and grind the wheat. He does all this kindly for us,—so that Rollo and all

The Garden, etc.

The Garden-yard.

the other boys in the world, may have some breakfast. I think we ought to thank him."

Rollo did not say any thing, but he thought so too.

FICTITIOUS STORIES.

"FATHER, will you tell me a story?" said Rollo, one day.

Rollo's father was sitting on the platform, leading out to the garden-yard.* It was a pleasant summer evening, just before sunset.

"Shall it be a true story or a *fictitious* one?" said his father.

---

* They called it the garden-yard because it led out to the garden. You can see Jonas in the picture, wheeling out a load of weeds, along the path from the garden to the barn-yard.

"What is fictitious?" asked Rollo.

"A story that is not true."

"But it would be wrong for you to tell me any thing that was not true, would it not?" said Rollo.

"Do you think it would be certainly wrong?"

"Yes sir."

"Suppose you were coming along the yard, and were riding on my cane, and should come up to me and say, 'Papa, this is my horse. See what a noble horse I have got.' Would that be wrong?"

"No sir."

"Would it be true?"

"No sir,—It would not be a real horse."

"Now do you know why it would be right in this case for you to say it was a horse, when it was not?"

Rollo could not tell.

"I will tell you," said his father. "Because you would not be trying to *deceive* me. I could see your horse, as you call him, and could see that it was nothing but a cane. You would not be trying to deceive me, to make me think it was a real horse when it was not."

"No sir," said Rollo.

"If you should say any thing which is not strictly true and want to make me think it *is* true, that would be very wrong. That would be telling a lie. So it would be very wrong for me to tell you any thing which is not true, and try to make you think it is true. But it is not wrong for me to make up a little story to amuse you, if I do not try to deceive you by it."

"Would that be a fictitious story?"

"Yes."

"Well father, I should like to have you tell me a fictitious story."

"Well, I will tell you one. The name of it is, The Fly's Morning Walk." So Rollo's father took his little boy up in his lap, and told him the following fictitious story.

THE FLY'S MORNING WALK.

ONCE there was a little fly with broad thin wings and round body and two great eyes. When he waked up in the morning, he found he was standing on the wall, and he thought he would go and find something for breakfast.

He flew down upon the table and then crept along. First he found a little grain of sand, and said he, "I wonder if this is good to eat." So he reached out his long *proboscis* to it, and tried to taste of it, but

he found it was dry and rough and hard.
" Oh, *no, no, no,*" said he, "this is not
good to eat."

Then he walked along a little farther,
and came to some dust. And he said,
" I wonder whether this is good to eat."
So he reached out his long proboscis to it,
and tried to taste of it ; but he found it
was dry and insipid, and it stuck all over
the end of his proboscis, and he said, " Oh,
no, no, no, this is not good to eat."

Then he went along until he came to a
pin, and he said, " I wonder whether this
is good to eat," so he reached out his long
proboscis and tried to taste of it, but it
was smooth and hard and round, and he
could not taste of it at all. And he said,
" Oh, *no, no, no,* this is not good to eat."

Then he went round to the point of the
pin, and he said, " I wonder whether this
is good to eat," but as soon as he touched

his long proboscis to it, it pricked the end of it, and he started back and said, "Oh, *no, no, no,* this is not good to eat."

Then he went along a little further, and came to a crack in the table, and he said, "I wonder whether there is any thing here good to eat." So he reached down his long proboscis into it, and got it pinched in, so he cried out, "Oh, oh, oh, this is not good to eat."

Then he went along a little further, and by this time he began to be very hungry, and presently, he saw a very small thing lying on the table, and he walked up to it, and began to feel of it with his long proboscis, and found it tasted very sweet and good. It was a little piece of a sugar-dog, which a boy had dropped there, and he said, "Oh, *yes, yes, yes,* this is very good to eat." Thus at last the little fly found some breakfast.

WAKING UP.

ROLLO's father was a very kind father. He took very good care of his little boy. He had a little trundle-bed made for him to sleep in, and good warm clothes for him to wear, and besides he would very often talk to him very kindly and pleasantly.

Once Rollo's mother took cold and became sick. Her sickness increased for several days, until at last it became necessary for her to have a nurse come and take care of her.

That night Rollo was put to bed in another chamber, and his father came to hear him say his prayers and to bid him good night. He put his cheek down to Rollo's, and they both prayed, first one and then the other, that God would take care of them both, and forgive their sins,

9*

and give them good and holy hearts and prepare them for heaven.

Just before his father went away, he said,

"Rollo, I am going to sleep here with you to-night."

"Are you?" said Rollo.

"Yes; the nurse is going to take care of mother, and in an hour or two, I shall come here and go to bed. Now when the morning comes, if you will pull me, and wake me up, I will tell you a little story."

"Well," said Rollo, "I will."

Then his father took up the light to go away.

Rollo did not want to have the light taken away, and he said, "Father, are you going to carry away the light?"

"Yes,—would 'n't you?" said his father.

"No sir, I think I would'nt."

"Oh yes, I think I must take the light away, and you must shut up your eyes and go to sleep."

So Rollo laid his cheek upon the pillow, and shut up his eyes, though they quivered a little, because he was not sleepy, and pretty soon his father went away.

The next morning, little Rollo was awakened by some one rubbing him, and when he opened his eyes he found that it was his father, whose face was close to his upon the pillow.

"Rollo," said he, "I told you, last night that if you would pull me and wake me up, this morning, I would tell you a little story: but you kept asleep all this time, so I had to pull you and rub you and wake *you* up; was not that funny?"

Rollo smiled faintly, for he was not yet quite awake.

Pretty soon he opened his eyes wide, and looked around the room. He saw that the window-curtains were very light, and he perceived that it was morning. His father then put his face to his, and said these words. He was praying to Almighty God.

"Oh God, thou hast been in this room all night, watching and taking care of little Rollo and me while we have been asleep. We thank thee that thou hast kept us safely. Wilt thou take care of us all the day and make us kind to all in the house. Do not let Rollo be disobedient or obstinate or ungrateful or unkind to little Lucy; and make us all good and happy for Christ's sake, Amen."

Rollo was still and attentive while his father said these words. He wanted God to hear and do what his father asked.

"Rollo," said his father, a few minutes

afterwards, "what are you going to do all day to-day."

"Oh," said Rollo, " I am going to play."

"Where are you going to get your breakfast ?"

"Oh I am going to get it down stairs, in the parlor."

"But whose breakfast is that down in the parlor?   Is it yours?"

"No sir."

"Did you buy it with your money?"

"No sir."

"Shall you get it ready?"

"No sir, I do not know how to get the breakfast ready."

"Then it is not your breakfast ; it is all my breakfast; but as you have not got any breakfast of your own, I believe I will let you have some of my breakfast.   But what are you going to do for a house to live in all day?"

"Oh," said Rollo, "I am going to live in this house."

"But is this your house?"

"No sir."

"Isn't it yours? Did not you build it?"

"No sir."

"Did not you buy it?"

"No sir."

"And hav n't you got any house to live in?"

"No sir, not unless you let me live in yours."

"Well, if you have not any house to live in, I will let you live in mine to-day."

Just then Rollo pointed up to the wall, and said,

"See, there is a tiger on the wall,—It looks like a tiger."

His father looked up at the irregular lines on the wall, which had attracted his little boy's attention, but he could not see any thing that resembled a tiger.

"I don't see," said his father; "where is his *head*?"

"He has not got any head; it is not a tiger, it only looks like a tiger. It has got a tail."

"Well, where is his tail?"

"I — don't — know. I see a stag, too, and camel."

In a minute or two his father turned Rollo's face over gently towards himself, so that his attention should not be attracted by what he saw there. He wanted him to listen to what he was saying to him.

"Well, Rollo," said he, "whose clothes are you going to wear to-day?"

"Oh I am going to wear *my* clothes," said Rollo; "yours would be a great deal too big."

" Have you got any clothes ?"

" Yes, sir."

" Where did you get them ?"

" I — do n't — know," said Rollo,
hesitating.

"The clothes which you wore yesterday belong to *me*," said his father. " Have
you got any others ?"

" Yes, sir," said Rollo ; " I have got
some up stairs in the drawer."

" Well, those belong to me.   I paid for
them with my money, and I might sell
them or give them away at any time, if I
chose.   Have you not got any others ?"

" No, sir," said Rollo.

" Well," said his father, " I shall let you
wear those clothes of mine then.   I am
very glad I have got a house, and some
breakfast, and some clothes for my little
Rollo boy, since you have not got any of
your own.   But I think if I get a house

for you to live in, and breakfast for you to
eat, and clothes for you to wear, you
ought to be a very careful, faithful, obedient little boy."

ROLLO'S PRAYER.

Every night, when Rollo went to bed,
he said a prayer which his father had taught
him. It is an excellent plan for a boy or
girl to say their prayers, every night. For
you have probably done something wrong
during the day, and you ought not to go
to sleep until you are forgiven. Besides,
God has taken care of you through the
day, and you ought not to go to sleep till
you have sincerely thanked him, and asked
him to take care of you through the night,
while you sleep. I will tell you what
Rollo's prayer was, and I think you had

10

better learn it and say it every night before you go to sleep, unless you have already learned some other one.

The Prayer.

Now that another day is gone, and I lay down my head upon my pillow to rest, I come to thee, Almighty God, my Heavenly Father, to ask thee to forgive my sins and to take care of me this night.

I have done wrong a great many times, —and destroyed my own peace of mind, and made my father and mother unhappy, and displeased thee. I pray thee, O God, to forgive me for Jesus Christ my Savior's sake; and will thou keep my heart that I may do wrong no more. Help me, every day, to try to please thee more and more, so that I may be thy dutiful and obedient child while I live, and my soul be saved when I die.

And now wilt thou come and be near

my bed-side while I sleep, keep me safe
until the morning; and always, whether I
wake or sleep, whether I live or die, wilt
thou be with me, and love me, and take
care of me, forever, for Jesus' sake.

Amen.

It will do no good to say this or any
other prayer, unless you say it seriously
and sincerely, and are really sorry for
having done wrong, and resolved to do so
no more.

BUNNY.

A FICTITIOUS STORY.

ONCE there was a beautiful wood, and
in it many large trees. In one of these
trees was a large hole; the bottom of the
hole was covered with dry leaves and

moss. Here lived Mr. and Mrs. Squirrel with their five children, named Creep, Peep, Bushy, Grey and Bunny. They were good little squirrels, and might have been a very happy family, had not Bunny been discontented. She tried to make the others so too. She would very often crowd her brothers and sisters, and fret because she had not room.

One day their father and mother were away, running about in the woods, trying to find something for them to eat. The little squirrels were playing together very pleasantly, till Bunny pushed Creep against Peep, and then shoved Bushy, telling them to move, for she had not room. In truth, Bunny was often a very naughty squirrel, and made her father and mother very unhappy. Very often they would lie awake at night thinking how they should make her a better child, and kind and pleasant to her brothers and sisters.

When they came home, the day I have mentioned, from their ramble in search of something to eat, they saw that their children looked very sober and unhappy, and Creep, who was the oldest, told them how Bunny had behaved. Creep was a very good squirrel, and her parents could always believe her. She never tried to make her brothers and sisters seem more naughty than they were.

That night, Mr. and Mrs. Squirrel talked about Bunny before they went to sleep, and concluded they *must* put a stop to her naughty behavior.

The next morning, Bunny's father got up and asked her to go and walk with him. She went, and they walked in the beautiful wood. There were nuts, and acorns, and berries, and Bunny longed to eat as many as she wanted.

Presently, her father told her how very

*e** 10*

wrong she had behaved, and that he must punish her. So he took her up with his fore paw, and ran up a tree. The tree was very tall, and it was a good while before they got far up. Poor little Bunny was very much frightened. At last they came to a small, dark hole, just large enough for her to turn round in. Here her father put her in, and told her she must stay there. Then he went away and left her here alone, and she could hear her father's feet pat along the tree as he went down, and then the dry leaves on the ground rustle as he ran over them.

Dinner time came, and Bunny hoped her father would come with some dinner. But no,—he did not come. She began to cry, for she was hungry. She felt with her paw all round, and could only find one little acorn and some dried leaves. She looked out of the hole, but was afraid to go out, it was so high up.

She now began to feel very sorry. She knew how unkind she had been to her brothers and sisters. She cried, and thought if her father would come and take her home, she would not crowd and push and fret any more.

Supper time came, but she could not hear any one coming.

The sun set,—it began to grow dark, and the winds blew and whistled through the trees. At last down poured the rain, and it came into the hole, and poor little Bunny was completely wet.

Presently she thought she heard a scratching and a patting on the leaves, and then upon the tree; and very soon up came her father. He saw that little Bunny looked sorry. She told her father she would try and be a good, pleasant squirrel if he would take her home and give her some supper. So he took her up with his paw and down the tree they went, and soon got home to their very warm nest. Here was a fine supper of sweet acorns—and the family were all glad to see little Bunny again, and whenever she began to be naughty, she thought of the dark hole where she had been left alone and without supper, and she became a very good little squirrel, and was ever afterwards a great comfort to her parents.

THE RAFT.

Do you remember any thing about Jonas;—how they found him by the side of the road and brought him home. When Rollo's father found him, he meant to have sent him to the poor-house, where all poor boys are taken care of, but he kept him in his house a few days first, and he found that he was a very good boy. He had a great many faults, but he was a good natured, pleasant boy, and he was willing to learn, and so Rollo's father thought he would let him stay and live with him, and work for him.

Jonas was very industrious and faithful. Do you know what industrious means? Do you know what faithful means? He was kind too. He was very kind to Rollo. He used to help Rollo a great deal, and play with him, and tell him stories.

There was a beautiful brook very near the house which Rollo lived in. I have made you a picture of the elm yard, behind the house. By and by, I shall make you a picture of all the house, and the trees, and fields around it, and the brook, and then you will understand it all exactly. Now I can only tell you there was a brook, and Jonas used to take Rollo down to the brook sometimes, to play. The brook was wide and the water flowed slowly and smoothly, but it was not very deep. Jonas liked to be near the water. He had sailed over the seas, and he liked the water.

One day Jonas found two great logs on the shore of the brook. He rolled them into the water. Then he went up to the house and got some pieces of board, and a hammer and some nails. He gave Rollo the hammer and nails to carry, and he carried the boards. He walked back then to the pond. He floated the logs side by side, and nailed the boards across, and then he stood upon it and it bore him up on the water. Jonas called it his raft. Then he took a pole and pushed himself off from the shore and shouted "HURRAH, HURRAH."

Rollo stood upon the shore looking at

And they sallied away up towards the bridge.

And they sailed away up towards the bridge.

him, and Rollo too shouted "HURRAH, HURRAH."

Then Rollo said, "Let me get on and sail too."

"No," said Jonas, "not till I ask your mother if she is willing."

That day when they went home, Rollo asked his father and mother if they were willing that he should sail on Jonas' raft. His father said he would go down and look at it. When he came to the brook he was surprised to see such a good strong raft, and he said that Rollo might sail on it, if they would both be careful. Then Jonas got on before, and pushed with his pole, and Rollo sat behind and held on, and they sailed away up towards the bridge. You can see them in the picture. You can see the raft, and Jonas pushing with a pole, and Rollo holding on, and the brook and the bridge. Rollo and

f 11

Jonas had a great many good sails on this raft.

CONTRARY CHARLES.

Do you know what a contrary boy is? I will tell you. He is one who is never satisfied with what he has, but always wants something different. If I were to say to you, "Come James, and see what a pretty *picture* I have got here;" and you should say, "No, I don't want a picture, you said you would bring me a pretty book,"—that would be being *contrary*. If your father should bring you home a little cart to draw about the room, and you should say, "I don't want a cart, I don't like carts, I want a horse and whip, like William's;" that would be being very contrary.

Now I knew a little boy once, who was unhappy a great deal of the time, because he would not be pleased with the playthings he had, but always wanted another kind, or something else. This little boy had a very kind father and mother, who loved him very much, and who tried to make him happy. They bought him good clothes to wear: they gave him good things to eat whenever he was hungry, and they bought him a great many pretty playthings. But though they were so kind, this boy was sometimes so naughty as to cry when they gave him a new plaything, because he had wanted a bunch of jack-straws, perhaps; instead of a pretty box of wooden blocks. If they had bought him some jack-straws, he would have wanted the blocks or something else. Nobody liked to give Charles any playthings or sugar-plums or any thing, because they did not make him happy: and they did not make him happy because he would not be pleased, but always thought of something else which he fancied he would rather have.

One day, Charles' mother came into the room where he was playing, and said, "Charles, little brother William is going to walk with Susan; should you like to go too?"

"Yes," said he, "but I shall want to wear my new cap."

"But I told you the other day," said his mother, "that you could not wear it for a whole week, again, because you threw it upon the floor when you came in yesterday, instead of hanging it on its nail."

"Then I don't want to go," said Charles.

"Very well," said his mother, and calling to Susan, she told her she need not wait any longer.

"But I *shall* want to go," said Charles, beginning to cry.

"You must not go now," said his mother, "for you said you did not want to go, just because you felt contrary, and out of humor."

His mother then sat down to work. Charles, finding it was useless to cry, dried his tears, and began throwing his playthings about the room.

"Don't you do so," said his mother; "you will break that pretty box, and your white cards, with the pretty colored letters, will get soiled, and not fit to be used."

"I don't care if they do," said Charles; "it is not a pretty box, and I don't like the cards."

His mother rose, took away all his playthings, and left him sitting upon the floor, with nothing to do. As she took

11*

no notice of his cross looks, he presently went to the window, and stood on a little cricket, looking to see the horses and carriages passing, and soon he began to feel pleasantly again.

"Oh! mother," said he, "there are two beautiful little dogs in the street, and a little boy running after them. Oh! how I should like a little dog. Mother, will you buy me one?" and he ran to his mother and looked up in her face.

His mother laid down her work and took him in her lap. "What would you do with a dog," said she, "if you had one?"

"Oh! I should play with him; I would put some things in my cart, and tie the dog to it, and let him draw it to market; just like the dog in William's picture."

"But I am afraid," said his mother, "that if your father should buy you a dog, you would sometimes get out of humor with him, and then you would say it was an ugly dog, and you did not want it any more."

"No, I would not," said Charles; "I should always love my little dog."

"So you said, if I would buy you a new cap, you would be a good boy, and never give me any trouble about it, but yesterday you forgot your promise, and did not put it where it belongs; and to-day you have made me very unhappy by your bad temper. And you have displeased God too, for he was looking directly into your heart when you said you did not want to go with Susan, and saw that you were saying what was not true."

"But I will remember next time, if you will only get me a little dog."

Just then William came into the room with a large piece of cake in his hand, which a lady had given him. He went up to his brother, and breaking it in two pieces, offered him one of them.

"No, I want the other piece," said Charles.

"But I can't give it to you," said William; "I want it myself."

"Then I won't have any," said Charles, impatiently.

"Keep all the cake yourself, William," said his mother; "Charles must not have any, because he is not a good boy."

"But I do want some," said Charles, beginning to cry very loud. Then his mother went to the door, and calling Susan, told her to take Charles into the other room, and keep him there until he was perfectly pleasant and good-humored. So you see Charles lost a pleasant walk and a nice piece of cake, and after all, had to be sent away from his kind mother, just because he would be a contrary boy. Do you think he was happy?

The next afternoon, as these two little boys were playing in the yard, they looked up, and saw a carriage, drawn by two large white horses, stop at the door. It was their aunt's. She had brought her little son and daughter, named James and Mary, to spend the afternoon with their cousins. As soon as they were out of the carriage, they ran to their cousins, and all looked as happy as if they were expecting to have a noble good time; and so they were.

Their aunt went into the house, and the children played together out in the yard. When they were tired of that, they went into the mowing field, where the hay was spread to dry, and began to throw it upon each other. This they enjoyed very much till Charles began to cry, and say

they should not throw the hay upon him.
He wanted to *pelt* the others, but was not
willing to have them pelt him. So this
contrary boy spoilt the whole play, and
he cried so loud that his mother had to
call him into the house. When he was
gone, James lay down in the hay, and
told his sister and cousin to cover him up
in it. When he was hidden entirely, so
that they could not see him, he jumped
up suddenly, and ran to catch them with
an arm full of hay, to *pay* them for treating him so. They laughed very loud,
and were very happy, now they had no
one to disturb them with crying. They
were soon called in to tea.

Charles had not been very well in the
morning, and his mother was afraid to give
him as many strawberries in his milk as
she did the rest. So Charles began to
cry, and said he would not have any. His

mother then sent him out of the room, and did not allow him to return until his cousins had gone.

You see how many pleasant things he lost by being so contrary. His mother said she could not buy him a dog until he had learned to be a good, pleasant boy. His cousins said they did not want to go and see him again, for he spoiled their play; and when his mother went to see his aunt, she took William, but left Charles at home. She said she could not take him with her until he was willing to do as others wished to have him, and not always cry to have his own way. By and by, Charles learned that it was better to be pleasant all the time, and not get out of humor when things did not exactly suit him; and then every body loved him, for he was a good little boy in every other respect.

CHARLES was a little boy. One cold winter's morning his mother brought him down stairs. It was very early. She put him down on the carpet, before a bright, warm fire. Then she opened the shutters to see if it was light. Charles saw something white and shining upon the windows, and called to her and said, "Oh, mother, mother, how beautiful! See how the windows are painted all white. *There* is a mountain, and another — and — and I see another on the top of it; and there are some trees, and flowers — and —"

"Yes, they are very beautiful," said Charles' mamma, as she stood dressing her little boy.

"What makes it look so? it isn't light like day,—and oh! mother, see, there is a bright star in the sky!"

"It is not quite daylight yet; pretty soon it will grow lighter, and the little star will not look so bright, and then the sky will grow brighter, and it will be daylight."

"What is it now; is it night?"

"No, it is day-dawn."

"Day-dawn;—well, it's very pretty, I think, mother. O see, there's a cow! I think those are pictures painted on the window, a'n't they?"

"No, they are not pictures. Don't you know what they are?"

"I see something that looks like a horse that hasn't got any head, and some trees that haven't got any branches, and a great many more mountains and rocks. I think they are pictures, but they look white, just like snow."

"Well, Charles, the cold made those pictures. We call it frost on the windows, and it came last night while we were all

12

asleep. It was very cold indeed last night, and a great many things froze very hard. Now hark, what do you hear?"

"Hark. I hear something that ticks just like a watch. What is it?"

"It is the cold frost, which has frozen some water in the tumbler. Last night it was water, and I drank some of it. Now look here; it is ice, and it looks very beautiful. See all those little marks and spots. Those are little bubbles. Now it goes *click, click,* again. See how hard it is; I cannot break it with my finger."

"Mother, will the frost stay all day on the windows, or go away when it is daylight?"

"Not when it is daylight, but when the room is warm. There is a good bright fire in the grate, and it will make the room warm, and by and by the sun will rise out of doors and shine on the glass and warm it, and the frost will melt. Then it will be water, and run down in drops."

"Well, I think it is very pretty frost, and I don't think I could make such horses, and trees, and cows."

SHOOTING A BEAR.

ONCE there was a foolish man, who was always afraid of bears. He was always afraid there were bears in the woods around him, and that they would come and eat him up.

One day he thought he would take his gun and go out and shoot a bear. So he took down his gun, and put in some powder to load it, and then he put in some paper to keep the powder in, and then he put in a bullet over that. The bullet was a round, heavy thing, like a round stone.

He put another piece of paper in next, to keep the bullet down. How do you suppose he got the paper down to the bottom of his gun? Why, he had a long slender iron, which he called his ramrod, and he pushed the paper down with his long slender ramrod. Then he pulled the ramrod out, and slid it into its proper place by the side of his gun.

Did you ever see any gunpowder? When you set it on fire, it flashes up very quick. There is a picture of some boys burning gunpowder in Rollo Learning to Talk. If the gunpowder is in a close place when it is set on fire, it bursts out violently, and makes a noise. This man's gun was a close place, and he expected that when he should see the bear, he should point his gun at the bear, and then set fire to the powder down in the bottom of his gun, and that the powder would flash and burst out, and drive out the round heavy bullet, and make it *whiz* through the air very swiftly, and go into the bear and kill him.

But how do you think he was going to set fire to the powder which was away down in the bottom of his gun, under the paper and the bullet? I will tell you how. There was a little hole, a very little one, in the side of his gun, opposite where the powder was, and he put a little powder into that hole. The name of the hole is the touch-hole. Close by that hole there were some things fixed which would strike together and make sparks. They would strike together when he pulled a little thing. The little thing he pulled was the trigger. So that when he should be all ready, and should have the gun pointing at the bear, he would only pull the trigger, and that would make the flint and

*f** 12*

steel strike together, and that would make
sparks, which would fall upon the powder
in the little touch-hole, and it would burn
in, quick, with a flash, and set the powder
in the gun on fire, and that would drive
the bullet out and make it whiz through
the air and kill the bear. That is the
way the man expected to shoot. That is
the way they always shoot.

Just before he was ready to shoot, he
always had to pull back the flint, so as to
get the flint and the trigger in the right
place, and when he did this it would say
click. This would be *cocking* his gun.
Then it would be ready to fire.

When the gun was all ready excepting
being cocked, the man put it on his
shoulder and went off into the woods
He looked all about him, but for a long
time he could not see any bear. At last
he saw a strange looking thing up in a
tree, among the leaves.

"I wonder," said he, "if that is not a bear."

It looked rather strangely, and he could not tell what it was if it was *not* a bear; so he thought he might as well shoot it. He accordingly took down his gun from his shoulder, and pulled back the flint and heard it say *click*. Then he pointed the gun up towards the strange looking thing in the tree, and he pulled the trigger. *Crackle* went the sparks, *flash* went the powder in the touch-hole, *pop* went the gun, *whiz* went the bullet through the air, and the man looked, expecting to see the bear fall down dead from the tree.

Instead of that he could see, when the smoke cleared away a little, that the strange looking thing appeared exactly as it did before. He went round a little to see it better, and what do you think it was? Why, it was only a crooked branch of the tree.

"Ah," said he, "I made a mistake. I ought to have waited until I saw whether it moved. Bears move. Next time I will not fire at any thing unless it moves."

So he went along a little farther, looking around on all the trees. At last he saw something upon a tree, moving; he thought that must be a bear. So he took his gun down quick off of his shoulder, and he pulled back the flint and it said *click,* and he pointed the gun up into the tree, and then he pulled the trigger. *Crackle* went the sparks, *flash* went the powder in the little touch-hole, *pop* went the gun, *whiz* went the bullet through the air, *puff* went the smoke, and the man looked, expecting to see the bear fall down dead from the tree.

Instead of that what do you think he saw? Why, it was nothing but a little squirrel, with a long bushy tail, running away on a limb of the tree, as fast as he could go. What the man saw moving was only the tip of his tail; the rest of him was round behind the tree, and he thought it was a bear round there.

"Ah," said the man, "I made another little mistake. Bears are black. This squirrel's tail is gray. I must not fire at any thing again unless it is *black*."

So he walked along, looking about him carefully, and up into all the trees. By and by he saw something moving. He looked up and saw that it was black. It was the little tip of a black thing; he could only see a little of it. The rest was round behind the tree.

"Now," says the man, "I *know* I have found a bear; for it is black, and bears are black."

So he loaded his gun and got it all ready. *Click*, said the lock when he cocked it. He pointed up towards the tree. In a minute he pulled the trigger,— *flash* went the powder in the touch-hole, *pop* went the gun, *whiz* went the bullet through the air, and the man look-ed, expecting to see the bear fall down dead from the tree.

Instead of that, what do you think he saw? Why, it was only a little black-bird, flying off through the branches as fast as he could go. The black thing which the man saw moving was only the blackbird's tail, *projecting* out from be-hind the tree, and he thought it was a black bear round there.

"Ah," said the man, "I made a mistake again. Bears are *large*, as well as black. This was very *little*. I must not fire at any thing again unless it is large as well as black."

So he walked along, looking about him

carefully, and up into all the trees. By and by he saw something very strange. It was a little way up a tree, clinging to a branch. It was partly hid by the leaves, so that he could not see it very well, but he knew that it was black, and it was large, and it was moving.

"Now," says the man, "I am certain I have found a bear, for it is large and black, and bears are large and black. Besides, it moves."

So he loaded his gun and rammed down the bullet with his ramrod, and pulled back the flint. It said *click*. Then he knew that all was ready. He was sure of his bear this time, and he determined to drag him home by the ears.

He pointed his gun up at the large black thing and pulled the trigger. *Flash* went the powder in the touch-hole, *pop* went the gun, *whiz* went the bul-

let through the air, and the man looked,
expecting to see the bear fall down dead
from the tree.

Instead of that a man came rushing out
of the bushes, calling out,

"Halloa there,—what are you shooting
my coat for?"

The man was at first so astonished that
he could hardly speak. Presently he
said,

"Who are you, sir?"

"I am a wood-cutter. I came out here
to cut wood, and I hung my coat on the
tree; now you have shot a hole through
it!!"

"Is that your coat?"

"Yes."

"I thought it was a bear."

"A bear!!" said the wood-cutter with
astonishment.

"Yes, I thought there were bears in

the woods, and that they would come out and eat me up; so I came to shoot one."

"You silly man," said the wood-cutter. "There are no bears in the woods near such towns as we live in. Besides, if there were, they never would come out of the woods and eat people up. Nobody is afraid of bears but silly little children."

———————

JACK HILDIGO.

Jonas used to sit down with Rollo very often and amuse him by telling him stories. The story which Rollo liked the best was the story of Jack Hildigo. The story of Jack Hildigo was a very curious one. The reason why I put it in this book is because it is very hard to read right, and you must read it aloud and distinctly till you learn to read it well.

13

When Jonas told this story they called it *playing* Jack Hildigo. It took several children to play it well. Sometimes when John and Samuel, who lived in another house, came over to play with Rollo, they would all sit down together, on the platform, in the garden-yard, and have a fine time playing Jack Hildigo.

Jonas would begin telling the story thus, the other children sitting all around him :—

"Once there was a boy, and his name was Jack Hildigo. One day he went round behind his father's house, and found there a great hole leading under the house. So he thought he would go into that hole, and see what was there. He went in under the house, but he found nothing. So he stood there, and began to growl like a bear, so,

"U-r-r, u-r-r, u-r-r."

Here Jonas, who was telling the story, said, U-r-r, u-r-r, u-r-r, growling as much as he could like a bear.

"Presently there came along a large turkey, saying, Gobble-gobble-gobble. And the turkey said, 'I wonder what there is in that great black hole.' And the turkey said, 'Hark! I hear a strange noise in that great black hole, something growling like a bear. I wonder what that is that is growling like a bear.'

"So the turkey walked along and looked in, and he said, 'Oh, it is nothing but Jack Hildigo. I am not afraid of Jack Hildigo. I will go in and gobble, while he growls like a bear.'

"So the turkey went in and stood by the side of Jack Hildigo; and the turkey said, Gobble-gobble-gobble, and Jack Hildigo growled like a bear, so."

Jonas would say, U-r-r, u-r-r, u-r-r, growling like a bear, and Rollo would say, Gobble-gobble-gobble, gobble-gobble-gobble, gobble-gobble-gobble, three times and no more. This would make Rollo laugh. Then Jonas went on with the story.

"By and by there came along a duck, a waddling, quacking duck. And the duck said, 'I wonder what there is in that great black hole.' And the duck said, 'Hark! I hear a strange noise in that great black hole, something growling like a bear. I wonder what that is that is growling like a bear.'

"So the duck walked along and looked in, and he said, 'Oh, it is nothing but Jack Hildigo and a turkey. I am not afraid of Jack Hildigo.' So the duck went in and stood by the turkey, and said, Quack-

quack-quack, and the turkey said, Gobble-gobble-gobble, and Jack Hildigo growled like a bear, so."

Here Jonas would say, U-r-r, u-r-r, u-r-r, and Rollo would say, Gobble-gobble-gobble, gobble-gobble-gobble, gobble-gobble-gobble, and John would say, Quack-quack-quack, quack-quack-quack, quack-quack-quack, all together, three times and no more. Here Jonas would go on with the story.

"By and by, there came along a dog, a large dog, a large black dog, with a bone in his mouth. And the dog said, 'I wonder what there is in that great black hole.' And when he came nearer, he heard a noise. And he said, 'Hark! what noise is that? It is something growling like a bear.' So he walked along carefully, but

13*

when he got near the hole he said, 'Oh, it is only Jack Hildigo and a turkey and a duck! I am not afraid of Jack Hildigo, or the turkey or the duck. I will go in and bow-wow-wow.' So he went in and stood by the side of the duck. And the dog said, Bow-wow-wow, and the duck said, Quack-quack-quack, and the turkey said, Gobble-gobble-gobble, and Jack Hildigo growled like a bear, so."

Here Jonas would say, U-r-r, u-r-r, u-r-r, growling like a bear, and Rollo would say, Gobble-gobble-gobble, gobble-gobble-gobble, gobble-gobble-gobble, and John would say, Quack-quack-quack, quack-quack-quack, quack-quack-quack, and Samuel would say, Bow-wow-wow, bow-wow-wow, bow-wow-wow, three times and no more. This would make them all laugh, and then James would go on with the story.

"In the yard of that house was a pig. He was lying down with his nose in the mud. And after lying there some time, he thought he would get up and take a walk.

"So he walked along till he came round behind the house, and he saw a great hole in the wall. And he said, 'I wonder what there is in that great black hole.' And when he came nearer, he heard a noise, and he said, 'Hark! what noise is that? It is something growling like a bear.' So he walked along carefully, but when he got near the hole, he said, 'Oh, it is only Jack Hildigo. I am not afraid of Jack Hildigo. I will go in and grunt while he growls like a bear.'"

When Jonas got as far as this, in telling the story one day, he stopped and said he could not go any farther, for there was nobody to play pig. But he said if he could only get four or five more boys some time, he could tell a good deal further, and they should have a great deal more fun.

This is the end of the story about Jack Hildigo.

HOW TO TREAT A KITTEN.

THERE was once a boy named James, and one day his father came home and said, "James, I have got something for you."

"What is it, father?" said James.

"Oh, I will show it to you presently," said his father.

"Where is it?" said James.

"It is in a little basket, which I left out in the other room."

So when James' father had put away

his hat and whip, he went out into the other room, and presently came in bringing a basket in his hands, which he was holding carefully by the handle.

"Oh, let me see, let me see," said James; and he came up to his father and began to pull down the basket.

This was wrong, for children ought never to attempt to pull any thing away from their father. It was foolish too, as well as wrong, for James could not succeed in pulling it away. The more he pulled, the higher his father held up the basket, until at last his father told him to let go. He obeyed.

Then his father held the basket down low. He put it in a chair, and James stood by the side of it. He saw that there was a cloth spread over the top of it and tied round the basket. James' father untied the string, and unwound it, and then carefully lifted up the cloth, and James looked in and saw there a beautiful gray kitten.

The kitten appeared afraid; she curled down into a corner of the basket, and looked up as if she was frightened.

"Oh, father," said James, "let me take her out."

"Well," said his father, "but do it carefully."

So James put his hands in to take up the kitten; but when she saw them coming, it frightened her more, and she jumped up to the top of the basket, and then leaped out upon the chair, and from the chair to the floor. She ran along the floor. At the same instant, James ran after her, holding out his hands, saying, "Oh, catch her, catch her." His father only turned round quietly and shut the door. He was much wiser than James, for James' bustle and noise only made the kitten more frightened, while his father quietly did what would effectually keep the kitten from running away.

"Now, James," said his father, "let the kitten stay there under the table a minute or two, while I tell you something. You see how frightened she looks. She is afraid you will hurt her. Now if you treat her very gently and kindly for a few days, and do not try to catch her at first, she will soon find out that you are her friend, and she will not be afraid of you. She will let you take her and play with her as much as you please. But if you handle her roughly, or tease her in any way, she will be always wild."

Then James' father went away.

James stood a minute or two looking at his kitten, and then he thought he would go and catch her. So he walked along towards the table, and then stooped down to take up the kitten, but she suddenly turned round and ran under the chairs, and hid behind a basket, in one corner of the room.

James ran after her. He pulled away the basket, and saw the kitten for an instant crouching in a corner of the room, staring wildly at him, and evidently very much terrified. The moment she found that the basket was taken away, and that she was exposed again, she started off, ran directly across the room, towards a large clock which was in the opposite corner and squeezed under it.

James now did not know what to do. He could not move the great heavy clock. He put his face close down to the floor and looked under, and he could just see the kitten's two shining eyes there, but he could not reach in, to take her.

"Ah," said he at last, "I know what I can do. I can go and get father's cane, and then I can *poke* her out." So he went out into the entry and got the cane, and came back and began to thrust it under and behind the clock. The poor kitten was much more frightened to hear this thumping around her, and to feel the great stick punching her sides; so presently she darted out, ran across the room, and out through the door which James had left open.

James followed her, brandishing* his cane. When he got to the entry, he found that the kitten was half way up stairs. He immediately began to go up as fast as he could, but she could go faster. She leaped up from step to step, then ran along the passage way at the top

* Brandishing it means holding it up as if he were going to strike her.

14

until she reached the door leading to the
garret, which James saw, to his chagrin,
was open a very little.

Do you know what chagrin means? It
means the feeling James had when he saw
that the garret door was open. What
sort of a feeling do you think that was?

The kitten squeezed through the open-
ing of the garret door, and disappeared.
James opened the door wide, and went
up nearly to the top of the garret stairs,
and looked into the garret. It was rather
dark there, and the boards looked loose
on the floor, and there were a great many
boxes and barrels there, and James was
afraid to go in. So he stood there and
called, "Kitty, kitty, kitty." But the kitten knew him by this time too well to
come.

Now James began to be sorry that he
had not taken his father's advice, and

treated his kitten more gently and kindly. He was afraid she was lost, and that he could never get her again.

That night, at tea time, when his father had heard all about it, he reproved James for his harsh and cruel treatment of his kitten, and told him that he thought he deserved to lose her entirely.

"Do you think I *shall* lose her entirely?"

"No," said his father, "not this time. I think I can get her out of the garret."

"How?" said James.

"Why, by kindness and gentleness. I shall draw her out by doing exactly the opposite to what you did to drive her in. But I do not believe it will do any good. I do not think you will ever treat her kindly enough to make her trust you."

James promised that he would; but his father knew that he did not always keep his promises.

That evening, James' father poured a little milk into a saucer, and he and James carried it up garret and put it upon the floor, and then came directly down again. The next morning they went up to look at it, and found that the milk was gone. They then brought down the saucer, filled it again, and carried it back. They stopped a minute to look round for the kitten, and presently they saw her behind a barrel. James wanted to go and catch her, but his father would not let him. His father said, "Poor pussy, poor pussy," in a gentle, soothing tone, and put the saucer down where she could see it, and then led James away down stairs. When he went out that morning he forbid James going to the garret till he came home.

At noon they carried some more milk up, and the kitten came out a little way towards them.

" There," said James' father, " do you not see the effect of kindness ?"

He then put the saucer down, and went back with James a few steps, and stood still. The kitten came up to the saucer and began to drink the milk.

" *Now* let us go and catch her," said James.

" No," said his father.

After the kitten had drunk all the milk, she ran back behind the barrel, and James and his father came down stairs.

The next time they went up, they stood close by the saucer, and the kitten came up slowly and cautiously. James' father gently stroked her back while she was feeding, and James thought he was certainly going to catch her then. But he did not ; he let her drink the milk and then go back behind the barrels.

g * 14*

"Why, father, are you not *ever* going to catch her?" said James.

"Yes," said his father, "when the proper time comes;" and they went down stairs.

The next time they came, the kitten came running out to meet them, and they held the saucer down. When she came near, James' father reached out his hand, and took her up gently, and said, "Now we will carry her down stairs."

"Let *me* carry her," said James.

"Well, you may," said his father; "but you must hold her very carefully." So James took the kitten, and his father took the saucer, and they went down stairs. They put the kitten and the saucer under the table, and pretty soon, though she seemed rather frightened at first, she began to drink. James' father forbid his touching her or doing any thing to her all day.

Thus in a few days the kitten became considerably tame, and would let James play with her, but he soon began to handle her roughly again. He would pull her by the tail, and carry her around under his arm, and try to make her stand up on her hind legs, and do a great many other things, which he thought was very good fun for him, but which were very terrifying or painful to her. The kitten became very much afraid of him. She would never let him play with her, or catch her, if she could possibly get away, and often in struggling to get away she would scratch his hands. Thus the kitten hated James, and James soon began to hate the kitten.

"She is a cross, ugly, good for nothing old puss," said he one day.

"Very well," said his father, "then I will take her out of your way."

So his father got the basket and put her gently in it, and he spread the cloth over it, and tied it down; James stood by looking sorrowfully.

"What are you going to do with her, father?" said he.

"I am going to take her out of your way. She shall never trouble you any more."

Then James' father put on his hat, and took the basket and walked away.

Some months afterwards James went to see Rollo. He found Rollo out on the platform, in the garden-yard. You remember the picture of the garden-yard. You can see the platform in the picture, if you look back.

When James arrived at the house, and went through to the yard to see Rollo, he found him playing horses. He had a little

wooden cart, very small, with a string tied
to it, and was trotting about on the platform. And who do you think he had in
the cart for a driver? Why, it was a little *gray kitten!* She was lying down in
the cart with her fore paws resting on the
front of it, and her chin resting on her
fore paws, and she seemed to enjoy her
ride very much. She looked so funny
that James could not help laughing.

"Oh, what a beautiful kitten!" said he.
"I wish I had such a kitten. I had one
once, but she was not such a tame, good
kitten as that,—she was an old, cross,
ugly, good for nothing puss. She did
nothing but scratch me."

Now it happened that this was the very
kitten which James had, though James
did not know it. His father had come
and given it to Rollo. Rollo called her

Ooty, and he made her gentle and tame by treating her kindly.

OVERBOARD.

Do you recollect what you read about Jonas' raft in another part of this book? One day, when Jonas was going down to the brook with Rollo, there was the following *dialogue* between Rollo's father and mother.

Mother. I am afraid to have Rollo sail with Jonas on that raft, as he calls it. I am very much afraid he will get in, some day.

Father. I presume he *will* get in.

Rollo's mother looked surprised. She thought it was strange that his father should let him go on the water, when he thought he probably would fall in.

Father. Perhaps I ought rather to say I think it not improbable that he will get in.

Mother. Why then do you allow him to go?

Father. Because the water is not deep, and with Jonas with him, who is a strong and a faithful boy, I think he cannot be hurt; and if he should grow careless and inattentive, and fall off of the raft, it would do him a great deal of good.

Mother. What good would it do him?

Father. It would make him more careful in future; and besides, an actual plunge into the water where it is deep enough to frighten a boy, will teach him more of the nature of water than an hour's talk to him about its properties. A fall off of Jonas' raft may, not very improbably, be the means of saving his life, by making him careful, when he shall be exposed to real danger.

Rollo's father was right; Rollo did fall off. One day, when he and Jonas were sailing up towards the bridge, Jonas was standing behind pushing, and Rollo was sitting on before. Rollo took up a long stick which was on the raft, and thought he would stand up and push too. Jonas stood with his back to him and did not see him. Rollo pushed his stick down into the water, but the bottom was farther off than it seemed to be, and leaning over he lost his balance, and away he went all over into the water. In an instant Jonas plunged in after him, and dragged him out upon the bank. The raft, left to itself, floated down the stream.

Rollo's mother put on dry clothes, and when Rollo was warm again she said,

"Perhaps now you think I shall forbid your going down to the brook again, but I shall not. You may go and sail again whenever you please."

Leaning over he lost his balance, and away
he went all over into the water.

She knew that his experience would make him careful in future, without any censure from her.

OLD THINGS AND NEW THINGS.

WHICH is the prettiest, an *old* thing or a *new* thing? Oh, a *new* thing to be sure, you say. A beautiful new book, fresh from the bookstore, is a great deal prettier than an old, worn out, tattered book, that you have had a great while.

Now there is one great mistake that small boys very often make. They think that books and other things become old and worn out, only because they have had them a long time; but that is not the reason. I have seen a great many books, beautiful books too, full of pictures, and they had been kept a great many years, and yet they were not old and worn out. They looked just as well as when they were first bought. Now I am going to explain to you here how you may keep your things so that they shall not become old and worn out.

Suppose your father should bring you home a beautiful book with a red morocco cover, and full of pictures. It looks new and beautiful. Now look at the cover a moment. Do you suppose the cover is red all through? Suppose any body should cut the corner off of the cover, should you expect that it would be red *all through* where they cut it? It would not. It is only red outside. The red is very thin, very thin indeed, spread all over the outside of the cover. You might take a knife and scrape it off in a little spot, and see that it is very thin, and that it is some other color underneath. Perhaps somebody will take some old book which is not good for much, and show you what I mean. You must not try it upon any good books.

Now suppose you should lay your red morocco book down upon the floor, and push it along, the floor would rub off a little of the red morocco. And then suppose that the next day you should lay it down on the stone steps, the rough stone would wear off more of the red morocco. And then suppose that you should lay it down open upon the table, or floor; a little dust from the table or floor would stick to the leaves, and spoil their whiteness. And then suppose you should let your book fall from a chair; it would bruise one of the corners, and bend it up a little. So if you go on a great many days, rubbing your book upon the floor,

h*   15*

and throwing it about, and tumbling the leaves, after a short time the beautiful red color of the cover would be worn off in spots, and the white paper would get soiled, and the corners very much bruised, and the book would begin to look old and tattered and torn. It would become an old, worn out book, not because you had kept it so long, but because you had used it roughly.

SELLING A BOY.

ONCE there was a man who was very poor. He had to work very hard to get money; but he found it very hard to get money enough to buy bread for himself, and his wife, and his little boy. So he thought he would go and see if he could not sell his little boy. He took him up

in his arms and went out into the street,
and walked along until he came to a shoemaker's shop. He thought that perhaps
the shoemaker would like to buy him.

So he stopped and looked in at the
window, and said,

"Shoemaker,—Mr. Shoemaker,—do
you want to buy a little boy?"

And the shoemaker said, "Is it a good
little boy?"

And the man said, "Yes, he is an excellent little boy; he always obeys me
exactly, and he is kind and gentle, and
not troublesome, and he tries to do right;
if you buy him, by and by, when he grows
up, he can work with you, and help you
make shoes."

"Well," said the shoemaker, "I will
give you a dollar for him."

"A dollar," said the man, thinking,
"shall I take a dollar for my little boy?

Then I should go home alone, and have nobody to play with me, and get up in my lap, and hear me tell stories. No, no, no, I will not sell my little boy for a dollar." So he walked on.

Presently he came to a carpenter's shop. He stopped at the window and said,

"Carpenter,—Mr. Carpenter,—should you like to buy a little boy?"

"A little boy!" said the carpenter; "what sort of a boy is he?"

"Oh," said the man, "he is an excellent little boy. I love him very much, but I have to sell him because I want some money to buy me some bread. But he is a good boy. He is obedient and faithful, and when he grows up he can help you saw boards and drive nails. The shoemaker offered me a dollar, but I could not sell him for a dollar."

"Well," said the carpenter, "I will

give you *ten* dollars for him, for he looks like a pretty good boy."

"Ten dollars," said the man, thinking, "ten dollars. Shall I sell my little boy for ten dollars? That would buy me a good deal of bread, but then I should not have any little boy. I should have nobody to come and meet me when I get home, or to sit still by my side when I am tired. No, no, no, I cannot sell my little boy for ten dollars." So he left the carpenter's and walked on.

The next place he came to was a mill. There was a great wheel spinning round and round in the water, and some carts filled with bags of wheat at the door. They were going to grind the wheat into flour. The miller came out to the door. His clothes looked white. The man said to him,

"Miller,—Mr. Miller, I have got a boy

to sell. Do you want to buy him?" As he said this he showed the miller the little boy who was in his arms.

"Is he a good boy, or a naughty boy?" asked the miller; "for I am sure I do not want to buy any naughty boys."

"Oh, he is a very good boy," said the man. "He does not cry, only when he hurts himself, and then he stops crying as soon as he can. He is not cross, or fretful, or disobedient, or troublesome. I know you will like him, and he will help you a good deal in your mill."

"Well," said the miller, "I think he is a good boy, and I should like a good boy in my mill very much. He could tie up the bags, and hold the horses at the door. I will give you a hundred dollars for him."

"A hundred dollars!" said the man; "that is a good deal of money." I could buy a *great many* loaves of bread with a hundred dollars. I could buy bread enough to last me a year, and as long as the money should last I could have a fine time resting from all my hard work. But then I should never see my poor little boy any more. And then perhaps he would not be happy with the miller. He may have to work too hard, and perhaps some of the horses which he would have to hold might kick him. No, I will not sell him to the miller for a hundred dollars, after all. I had rather carry him home, and work the harder."

So he left the miller and walked on. He thought that perhaps somebody would give him more money for his boy. He walked on a little way and came to a large, beautiful white house by the side of the road. It belonged to a rich gentleman, who was standing at the door.

He thought he would go and offer him to this rich gentleman. While he was hesitating, he looked into his little boy's face, and he was so pleasant, and looked so gentle and kind, that the man could not bear to sell him.

"No, no, no," said he, "I will not sell my little boy at all. I have kept him a good while, and taken care of him, and I love him very much. No, I will not sell him. I will carry him home, and work very hard to get bread for him to eat. And he will be kind, and dutiful, and obedient, and when I grow old perhaps he will take care of me. No, no, I would not sell him for a thousand dollars."

This is a fictitious story. It is written to teach children that if they are good, and kind, and obedient, their fathers will love them, and work hard, if necessary, to get them bread, and will not sell them, even if any body should offer them a thousand dollars.